You're My Hero, Charlie Brown!

You're
My Hero,
_____

— Charlie Brown!

Selected Cartoons from PEANUTS EVERY SUNDAY VOL.2

by CHARLES M. SCHULZ

FAWCETT CREST • NEW YORK

YOU'RE MY HERO, CHARLIE BROWN

This book, prepared especially for Fawcett Crest Books, a unit of CBS Publications, the Consumer Publishing Division of CBS Inc., comprises the second half of PEANUTS EVERY SUNDAY, and is reprinted by arrangement with Holt, Rinehart and Winston, Inc.

ISBN: 0-449-23851-2

Printed in the United States of America

36   35   34   33   32   31   30   29

CLOMP!

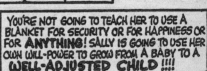

OF ALL THE STUPID **HABITS**, THAT BLANKET IS THE **STUPIDEST**! AND THAT'S ALL IT IS, JUST A **HABIT**! A STUPID **HABIT**!!

YOU'RE NOT GOING TO TEACH HER TO USE A BLANKET FOR SECURITY OR FOR HAPPINESS OR FOR **ANYTHING**! SALLY IS GOING TO USE HER OWN WILL-POWER TO GROW FROM A BABY TO A **WELL-ADJUSTED CHILD**!!!!

LIKE HER BROTHER?

SIGH

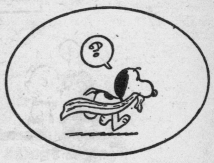

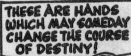

BUT THAT'S THE WHOLE IDEA, CHARLIE BROWN... THE ODDS NOW ARE REALLY IN YOUR FAVOR!

ONE OF THESE TIMES I MAY **NOT** JERK THE BALL AWAY! ONE OF THESE TIMES I MAY ACTUALLY HOLD ON TO IT!

I NEVER THOUGHT OF IT THAT WAY...

OKAY... YOU HOLD THE BALL, AND I'LL COME RUNNING UP, AND KICK IT!

AAUGH!

WHAM

I'M SORRY... THIS WASN'T THE TIME!

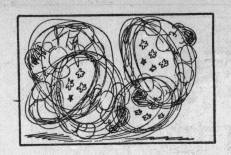

✿ POW! WHAM! ✿

BANG
WHAP! POW!
SOCKO!
OUCH! OOF!
LEGGO!
YIPE!

I CAN'T GET THAT STUPID KITE IN THE AIR! I CAN'T! I CAN'T!

OH, COME ON NOW, CHARLIE BROWN...THAT'S NO WAY TO TALK...

THE WHOLE TROUBLE WITH YOU IS YOU DON'T BELIEVE IN YOURSELF! YOU DON'T BELIEVE IN YOUR OWN ABILITIES!

IS THIS ALL YOU HAVE TO DO? ARE YOU GOING TO SPEND THE WHOLE DAY SLIDING BACK AND FORTH ON A PIECE OF ICE?!

DO YOU THINK THESE DAYS WERE GIVEN TO YOU TO WASTE? DOESN'T LIFE MEAN MORE TO YOU THAN THIS?!

IT ALWAYS COMES AS A SHOCK WHEN IT HAPPENS TO SOMEONE YOU KNOW...

DO YOU WANNA SEE A KID WITH A GREAT THROWING ARM?

THERE'S A KID WITH A GREAT THROWING ARM!

WELL, HOW DID THE SKIING GO?

I CAN TAKE IT OR LEAVE IT!

SKRITCH
SKRITCH
SKRITCH

SKRITCH SKRITCH
SKRITCH
SKRITCH
SKRITCH

SIGH

WHAT DO YOU HAVE THERE, CHARLIE BROWN?

I'VE WRITTEN A POEM..

REALLY? READ IT..

ALL RIGHT.. IT ISN'T VERY LONG..

SOME DAYS YOU THINK MAYBE YOU KNOW EVERYTHING...SOME DAYS YOU THINK MAYBE YOU DON'T KNOW ANYTHING...SOME DAYS YOU THINK YOU KNOW A FEW THINGS...SOME DAYS YOU DON'T EVEN KNOW HOW OLD YOU ARE.

YOU CAN'T THROW ME OUT OF MY OWN HOUSE!

I LIVE HERE, TOO, YOU KNOW! YOU'LL NEVER GET AWAY WITH THIS! DO YOU HEAR ME?!!

SHE DRIVES ME CRAZY! I'M SO MAD I FEEL LIKE I'M GOING TO EXPLODE!!

I DON'T HAVE TO STAND FOR THIS! I DON'T HAVE TO TAKE THIS FROM HER!

I'M GOING TO TELL HER OFF LIKE SHE'S NEVER BEEN TOLD OFF BEFORE!

SLAM!

WELL?

I HOPE YOU DON'T GET ANYTHING YOU WANT FOR CHRISTMAS!

PERHAPS YOU SHOULD
SEE A DOCTOR...

I NEVER THOUGHT SHE'D PICK UP THE SPARE!

OH, CUT IT OUT!

WELL, THEY ARE!

WHAT ABOUT THAT LITTLE KID LAST YEAR WHO WOULDN'T SAY HIS PIECE? HE WOULDN'T EVEN GET OFF HIS MOTHER'S LAP! HE WAS SCARED! HE WAS REALLY SCARED!

AND WHAT ABOUT THAT LITTLE BLONDE GIRL WHO STARTED TO CRY WHEN EVERYONE ELSE WAS SINGING? DON'T TELL ME THAT ISN'T WRONG!

I'M REVOLTING AGAINST CHRISTMAS PROGRAMS!!

LOOK...DO YOU SEE THIS? WHAT IS IT?

IT'S MY PART IN THE CHRISTMAS PROGRAM...I'M SUPPOSED TO MEMORIZE IT..

ALL RIGHT...NOW DO YOU SEE THIS? WHAT IS THIS?

IT'S A FIST!

"AND IT CAME TO PASS IN THOSE DAYS, THAT THERE WENT OUT A DECREE FROM CAESAR AUGUSTUS, THAT ALL THE WORLD SHOULD BE TAXED..."

I'LL NEVER BE ABLE TO MEMORIZE THAT PIECE! NEVER!!

I'M DOOMED!

OH, HI, CHARLIE BROWN.. SAY, HOW ARE YOU COMING ALONG ON YOUR PIECE FOR THE CHRISTMAS PROGRAM?

YOU KNOW, IF NONE OF US LEARN OUR PIECES, THERE WON'T BE ANY PROGRAM, WILL THERE? IF NONE OF US ARE ABLE TO MEMORIZE OUR PIECES, THEY...

"AND THERE WERE IN THE SAME COUNTRY SHEPHERDS ABIDING IN THE FIELD, KEEPING WATCH OVER THEIR FLOCK BY NIGHT."

THIS IS GOING TO BE A BLACK CHRISTMAS...

THIS IS A SCULPTURE WHICH STANDS IN THE LITTLE GARDEN JUST BEHIND THE HOUSE..

HERE I AM AGAIN POSING BY THE HOUSE

WILL THESE PICTURES BE WORTH A LOT OF MONEY SOMEDAY?

I DOUBT IT..

I DON'T SEE HOW ANYBODY CAN SAVE SOMETHING THAT WON'T BE WORTH A LOT OF MONEY SOMEDAY..

THUS ENDETH THE CROQUET GAME!

MORE PEANUTS®

☐ SING FOR YOUR SUPPER, SNOOPY
(selected cartoons from
The Beagle Has Landed, Vol. 3)   24403 $1.75

☐ SNOOPY, TOP DOG
(selected cartoons from
The Beagle Has Landed, Vol. 2)   24373 $1.75

☐ JOGGING IS IN, SNOOPY
(selected cartoons from
The Beagle Has Landed, Vol. 1)   24344 $1.50

☐ STAY WITH IT, SNOOPY!
(selected cartoons from
Summers Walk, Winters Fly, Vol. 3)   24310 $1.50

☐ PLAY BALL, SNOOPY
(selected cartoons from
Win a Few, Lose a Few, Charlie Brown,
Vol. 1)   23222 $1.75

☐ HERE'S TO YOU, CHARLIE BROWN
(selected cartoons from
You Can't Win, Charlie Brown, Vol. 2)   23708 $1.50

Buy them at your local bookstore or use this handy coupon for ordering.

COLUMBIA BOOK SERVICE, CBS Publications
32275 Mally Road, P.O. Box FB, Madison Heights, MI 48071

Please send me the books I have checked above. Orders for less than 5 books must include 75¢ for the first book and 25¢ for each additional book to cover postage and handling. Orders for 5 books or more postage is FREE. Send check or money order only.

Cost $_____   Name _____

Sales tax*_____   Address _____

Postage_____   City _____

Total $_____   State _____ Zip _____

* *The government requires us to collect sales tax in all states except AK, DE, MT, NH and OR.*

This offer expires 1 March 82

8186